Handling ADHD

by Carol Hand

Content Consultant
Melissa R. Dvorsky, PhD
Clinical Psychologist
Children's National Hospital
Assistant Professor of
Departments of Psychiatry &
Behavioral Health and Pediatrics
George Washington University

Handling *Health Challenges*

Essential Library
An Imprint of Abdo Publishing
abdobooks.com

abdobooks.com

Published by Abdo Publishing, a division of ABDO, PO Box 398166, Minneapolis, Minnesota 55439.

Printed in the United States of America, North Mankato, Minnesota.
052021
092021

THIS BOOK CONTAINS RECYCLED MATERIALS

Cover Photo: Shutterstock Images
Interior Photos: Shutterstock Images, 4, 14, 89, 90, 42; Gaudi Lab/Shutterstock Images, 8; Pavel Metluk/Shutterstock Images, 13; Africa Studio/Shutterstock Images, 21; iStockphoto, 22, 24, 27, 32, 36, 40, 65, 80; Red Line Editorial, 38; Wellcome Collection (CC BY 4.0), 46, 51; Dragon Images/iStockphoto, 56; Deepak Sethi/iStockphoto, 61; Monkey Business Images/Shutterstock Images, 68, 73; New Africa/Shutterstock Images, 77; Pure Radiance Photo/Shutterstock Images, 85; M. Spencer Green/AP Images, 95

Editor: Arnold Ringstad
Series Designer: Megan Ellis

Library of Congress Control Number: 2020948030

Publisher's Cataloging-in-Publication Data

Names: Hand, Carol, author.
Title: Handling ADHD / by Carol Hand
Description: Minneapolis, Minnesota : Abdo Publishing, 2022 | Series: Handling health challenges | Includes online resources and index.
Identifiers: ISBN 9781532194924 (lib. bdg.) | ISBN 9781098215231 (ebook)
Subjects: LCSH: Attention-deficit hyperactivity disorder--Juvenile literature. | Attention-deficit-disordered youth--Juvenile literature. | Attention-deficit hyperactivity disorder--Diagnosis--Juvenile literature. | Attention-deficit hyperactivity disorder--Treatment--Juvenile literature. | Health--Juvenile literature.
Classification: DDC 618.928589--dc23

Contents

Chapter **One**

Living with ADHD

Jake was diagnosed with attention deficit hyperactivity disorder (ADHD) when he was 12 years old. Before his diagnosis, he often felt out of control. School was especially hard. He couldn't sit still or pay attention. His teachers complained that he was interrupting class and talking to his friends instead of listening. Outside of class, his parents worried about him taking risks and getting hurt. His mom kept urging him, "Think before you act," but he couldn't seem to do it. He punched his friends and chased balls into the street without looking. One day, he jumped off the roof of his house because it looked like fun, and he broke his ankle. Shortly afterward, his mom took him to a psychologist, who diagnosed him with ADHD. Basically, that meant he was very impulsive, inattentive, and hyperactive. Jake knew

ADHD can affect a student's ability to pay attention in class.

all that—everyone kept telling him. He just hadn't realized there was a name for it.

Learning to Manage ADHD

After his diagnosis, Jake's life improved slowly but steadily. The pill he now took every morning made him feel calmer and slowed him down a bit. His mind felt clearer and he could think better. He was less tempted to do impulsive and dangerous things, and he was less likely to make his teachers mad by interrupting them and acting out in class.

His parents and older sister learned ways to better support him too. The whole family helped him set up a schedule, and everyone reminded him to follow it. That way, he got everything done, at least most of the time. He even made it to his appointments

Warning Signs of ADHD

If a parent or teacher notices that a child exhibits certain behaviors or symptoms over a long period of time, these may be considered warning signs of ADHD. These behaviors include inattention, or difficulty paying attention; hyperactivity, or excess activity; and impulsivity, or acting without thinking. They may interfere with the child's development or ability to function. Showing these warning signs does not necessarily mean a child has ADHD. A specific diagnosis must be made by a mental health professional.

on time—school, soccer practice, band practice, trumpet lessons, and of course his weekly visit to the psychologist. At first, he fought against seeing a psychologist. He didn't want people to think he was crazy or that he couldn't handle his own life. But Dr. Lopez turned out to be fun, and she was an amazing help in managing Jake's ADHD.

Keeping a Daily Schedule

Jake's life these days as a high school sophomore revolves around his daily schedule, which he updates conscientiously and keeps in his smartphone. Alarms constantly alert him to his next appointment. His days are fairly predictable, and his routine keeps him on track. Every day, Jake's alarm goes off at 6:00 a.m., and he wakes rested after eight hours of sleep. He still hates getting up, but he knows how important his routine is and does his best to stick to it. These days, his mom only has to wake him occasionally. Jake keeps his medication by his bed,

> "The good news is that, when you graduate from high school, you are going to know how to work through struggle. To me, that is the core of success."[1]
>
> *—Michael Riera, PhD, speaking to kids with ADHD*

Sticking to a schedule or routine can help students with ADHD manage the challenges of the disorder.

and he takes his pill first thing. Then, he goes for a run—it takes him 30 minutes to reach the park, take a lap around it, and dash home again. Building physical activity into his morning routine helps him burn off extra energy. This will make it easier to sit quietly once he gets to school. He takes a quick shower and then gets dressed.

During breakfast, Jake tells his family his schedule for the day. He is proud of this part of his day—only recently have his parents let him take charge of his

Time Management

Establishing good time management is key to living with ADHD, especially for busy middle and high school students. Getting enough sleep is vital, since a lack of sleep makes ADHD worse. Prioritizing is also critical. Teens have many activities and deadlines. Determining which is most important at any given time is essential. For example, if there are two term papers due soon, which should be written first? Meeting deadlines also means estimating how long each task will take and allowing enough time to complete that task. If the task is complex, it can be broken into smaller, more manageable parts. Procrastination, or waiting until the last minute to complete an assignment, is another common problem with ADHD. Setting small, achievable goals, such as reading for five minutes, can help with getting started on less desirable tasks.

Keeping appointments also requires time management skills. People with ADHD can make sure they know when and where the appointment is, know how long it takes to get there, and schedule enough time to make it. Electronic calendars can be a huge help with scheduling and time management. Recording all appointments and deadlines in a smartphone, and synchronizing the phone with other devices, can help people ensure they don't miss anything.

own schedule. As long as he stays organized and his life runs smoothly, his parents give him the freedom of responsibility for himself. This is a big step forward. After his diagnosis, his mother watched him constantly, telling him what to do and when to do it. Now he finally feels like he has some control over his

Conditions Associated with ADHD

Several behavioral conditions are closely related to ADHD. Specific learning disorder, or learning disability, involves difficulty with reading, writing, or math. The reading disorder dyslexia is the most common. One-third of people with a learning disability also have ADHD.[2] People with disruptive, impulse-control and conduct disorders show anger or aggression directed toward people or property. They may have trouble controlling their emotions, or they may break rules or laws. People with social communication disorder have difficulty using verbal and nonverbal language in social situations. People with autism spectrum disorder have difficulty with social interactions, nonverbal communication, and speech. The severity of these problems varies greatly from person to person.

own life, and he is determined to be responsible and keep that control.

School is better too. Jake's teachers are all aware of his ADHD diagnosis. Today, he has a math test. His math teacher lets him take it in a separate room, where Jake will be less distracted, and his teacher gives Jake extra time. His English teacher reminds him that he has a paper due tomorrow, and Jake assures her that he is working on it and will finish it on time.

Of course, Jake's life isn't perfect. Today at lunch, his friend Josh was being a jerk, making smart remarks and punching Jake on the shoulder as he tried to eat his lunch. Jake got mad and jumped up, ready to fight. The cafeteria monitor stopped the commotion and gave both boys a warning. Jake left lunch early and—following another of Dr. Lopez's suggestions—spent the last ten minutes of the period alone in the gym, taking his anger out on a punching bag. By his next class, he was calm again.

Right after school, Jake has a trumpet lesson with his band director, Mr. Ellis. Trumpet lessons are always fun, and he's getting pretty good. Mr. Ellis says that if he keeps up the good work and practices every day, he has a shot at getting a solo in the next band concert. That's definitely a goal to work toward, and it gives Jake a

"Many teens with ADHD find that the school environment does not suit their personality or maximize their natural talents. It is important for you to find your place in life and identify your strengths: Are you athletic? A good artist? Do you have musical talent? Are you good with computers? Find environments and activities that remind you of your strengths and allow you to experience success."[3]

—Children and Adults with Attention-Deficit/Hyperactivity Disorder's (CHADD's) National Resource Center on ADHD

good reason to stick to his routine. After his lesson, Jake runs around the track a couple of times before heading home to have dinner. He practices trumpet, finishes his English paper, and is in bed by 10:00 p.m. All in all, it's been a good day—better than he could have imagined before his ADHD diagnosis.

ADHD in Real Life

Jake is fictional, but his struggles—and his successful efforts to overcome them—represent life for many kids around the world. According to the latest national figures, released in a 2016 study by the Centers for Disease Control and Prevention (CDC), approximately 9.4 percent of US children had been diagnosed with ADHD. This included four million children ages six to 11 and three million ages 12 to 17. Some are diagnosed as young as age two. Boys are more than twice as likely as girls to be diagnosed with ADHD. These numbers have all increased since 2003.[4]

Worldwide in 2015, about 7.2 percent of kids 18 and under—approximately 129 million kids—had ADHD, according to researchers at Bond University in Queensland, Australia. The figure for adults was about 3.4 percent.[5] The number of ADHD diagnoses surged worldwide in the 2000s. Experts think some

The CDC is among the organizations that study the causes, symptoms, and prevalence of ADHD.

of this rise may be a result of better recognition and acceptance of ADHD. Others fear the condition may be overdiagnosed—that some people being diagnosed with ADHD do not really have it. But millions of children and adolescents do struggle with issues related to ADHD, and behavioral treatments and medications that are now available are helping them live normal, happy lives.

Chapter
Two

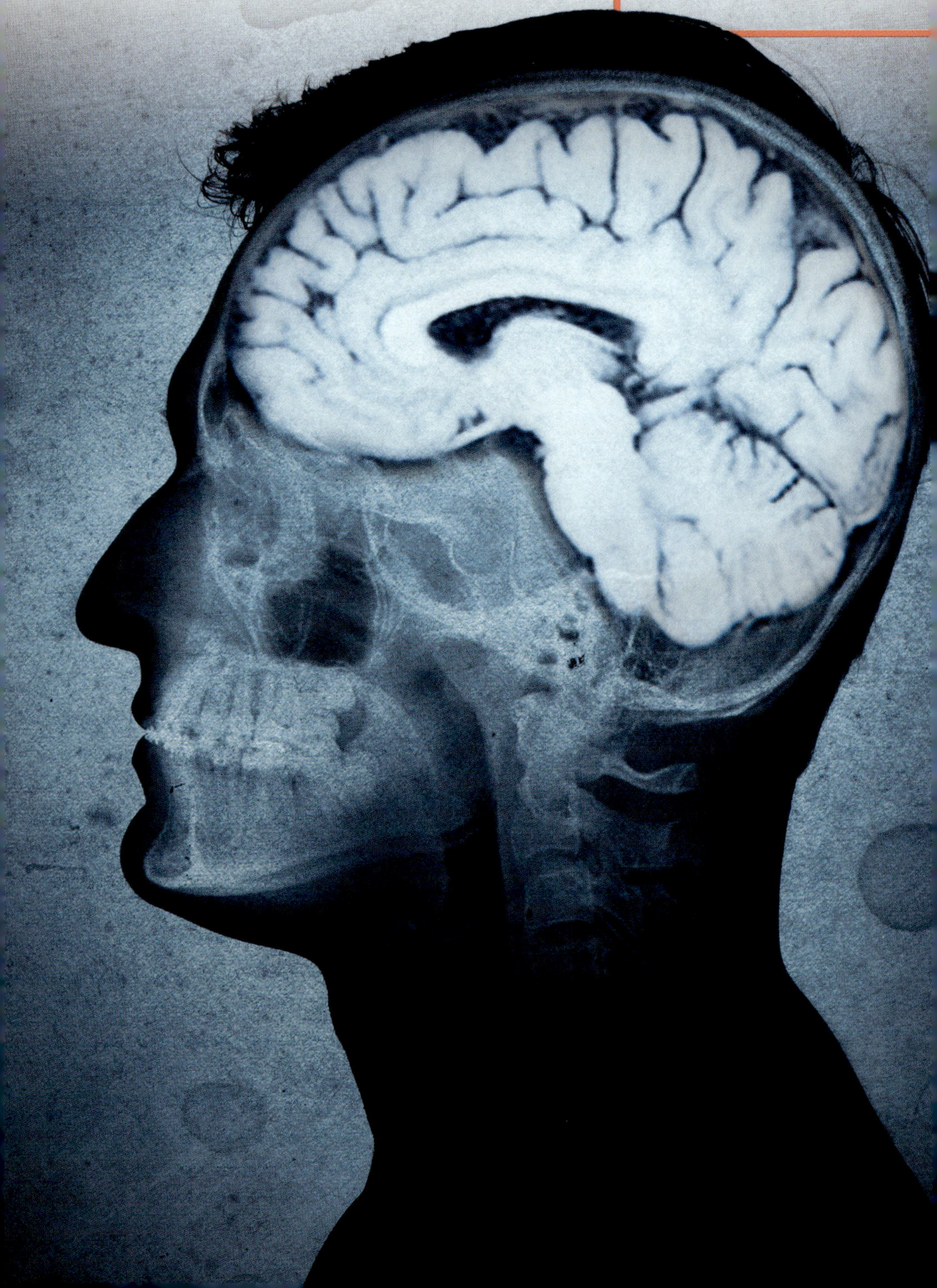

Causes of ADHD

ADHD is a neurobehavioral condition. That means it influences a person's behavior by affecting the way that person's brain processes information. Scientists are still actively researching the causes of ADHD. Most are convinced that the major cause of the condition is genetics; that is, ADHD is inherited from parents. Other things are also considered possible causes or risk factors. These include brain injury; exposure during pregnancy to environmental toxins, such as lead; alcohol or tobacco use during pregnancy; low birth weight; and premature delivery.

The Genetics Connection

There is strong evidence that ADHD is inherited. Children are more likely to have ADHD if one of their parents has it. As with most mental health disorders, scientists have not determined which gene

Whether the cause is genetic or environmental, the processes that create ADHD symptoms occur in the brain.

or genes are responsible for ADHD. Likely more than one gene is responsible. The one most studied is the DRD4 gene, which affects dopamine receptors in the brain. Dopamine is a neurotransmitter, or brain chemical, that helps regulate emotional responses and controls the feelings of pleasure and reward. A variation of the DRD4 gene occurs in some people who have ADHD. Scientists think it might be involved in causing the condition.

What Does Not Cause ADHD

Some people suggest that ADHD is caused by certain factors in the environment or family life. But there is no evidence that ADHD is caused by things such as food additives, allergies, immunizations, or lots of sugary snacks. There is also no evidence that it is caused by watching too much television or playing video games, or by social and economic factors such as poor parenting, poverty, or family problems. Many factors, including some on this list, might make ADHD symptoms worse in some people. But there is no evidence that they cause the condition.

Studies indicate that ADHD is based more than 70 percent on genetics.[1] Because causes likely include both genes and environmental factors, a parent with ADHD will not automatically pass it on to his or her child. Also, even if a child inherits genes that can lead to ADHD, those genes may never be activated, meaning the child may never develop ADHD. In one study, only one-third of children whose fathers had ADHD developed the condition. Because more boys than girls have ADHD diagnoses, some people assume the condition is sex-linked, but it is not. Mothers as well as fathers can have ADHD, and both can pass the genes on to their children. However, scientists know that ADHD is not totally caused by genetics, because the condition shows up in cases where no family history of ADHD exists.

Twin and Family Studies

Several lines of evidence from twin and family studies point to a genetic basis for ADHD. According to twin studies, if one identical twin has ADHD, there is an 82 percent chance that the other twin will have it as well. The likelihood for fraternal twins is only 38 percent. Finally, the biological families of adopted children with ADHD are more likely to have members with ADHD than are their adopted families.[2]

Other Factors

ADHD also has possible environmental causes. They include neurotoxic chemicals, or chemicals that poison the nervous system, including the brain. Lead and organophosphate pesticides are the most strongly correlated. Lead poisoning appears to affect children's ability to learn. It is also implicated in impulsivity, hyperactivity,

> "The first step in helping a person with ADHD is understanding the origins of the condition. By understanding that these origins typically include genetic factors, people can become more objective about the condition and its effects, and blame doesn't have to be placed on parents or the person with ADHD."[3]
>
> *—Kathleen Smith, PhD, licensed professional counselor*

and inattention. Lead is particularly common in older homes and schools. A 2009 study showed that children with ADHD have higher blood levels of lead than children without it. Organophosphates, which are pesticides commonly used on lawns and in agriculture, are thought to adversely affect nervous system development in children. One 2010 study showed that children with higher levels of organophosphates in their urine are more likely to have ADHD. Another showed that a mother with high levels of this pesticide in her urine is more likely to have a child with ADHD. These studies show a correlation, or link, but they do not definitively prove that organophosphates cause ADHD. Other chemicals that may be linked to development of ADHD are

Correlation vs. Causation

Some factors are linked, or correlated, to ADHD. For example, children with ADHD tend to watch more television and play more video games than children without it. However, this does not mean that watching television or playing video games causes ADHD. Children who have ADHD might simply be more attracted to those activities. That is, correlation is not the same as causation, or a cause-and-effect relationship. It is easy to show a correlation between two factors, such as when both increase at the same time. But it is much harder to prove that one factor causes the other. Scientists usually prove causation by doing controlled studies. They cannot manipulate a condition such as ADHD. Instead, they might compare two groups of families. The presence of ADHD in biological, but not adoptive, parents provides evidence that ADHD is caused by genetics. This represents causation, not just correlation.

industrial chemicals called PFCs, which are found in stain-resistant coatings and food packaging, and phthalates, which are found in some toys, food packaging, and cosmetics.

Mothers who smoke or drink alcohol during pregnancy also increase the risk that their unborn children will develop ADHD. Research has shown strong correlations, particularly with smoking, but so far it does not show proof of causation. A 2018 study showed a significant correlation between smoking during pregnancy and that child developing ADHD. Children of heavy smokers were more

ADHD and Bipolar Disorder

Children diagnosed with ADHD may have a greater risk of developing other conditions. One of these is bipolar disorder, which involves severe mood swings. People range from manic episodes characterized by highly energized, often elated, behavior to serious bouts of depression. In studies, anywhere from 9 to 35 percent of adults with bipolar disorder also have ADHD.[4] There is some overlap between ADHD and the mania, or manic symptoms, of bipolar disorder. During manic periods, people may have trouble keeping organized and staying focused on tasks. Doctors say these people may also have ADHD, and when people with these symptoms are treated for both disorders, they usually gain more control over their lives.

likely to develop the condition. Another 2018 study showed a strong correlation between drinking during pregnancy and the unborn child developing ADHD—specifically, the mother drinking at least four drinks occasionally or fewer drinks frequently.

However, a 2017 study showed no correlation between a mother's alcohol use and her unborn child's later development of ADHD. Children of drinking mothers were likely to develop some ADHD symptoms, but not enough to result in an ADHD diagnosis. Other complications of pregnancy and childbirth are also implicated in higher risk of ADHD. These include low birth weight, premature birth, and having a difficult pregnancy.

Studies have linked smoking in pregnant women with the development of ADHD in these women's children.

Finally, certain brain injuries or illnesses can cause ADHD because they affect areas of the brain associated with motor activity, impulse control, or other ADHD symptoms. These brain traumas might include blows to the head, brain tumors, strokes, or diseases such as encephalitis or meningitis. However, these conditions involve only a tiny percentage of ADHD cases and are not considered major risk factors.

Much is not yet known about the causes of ADHD. For example, although scientists believe ADHD is

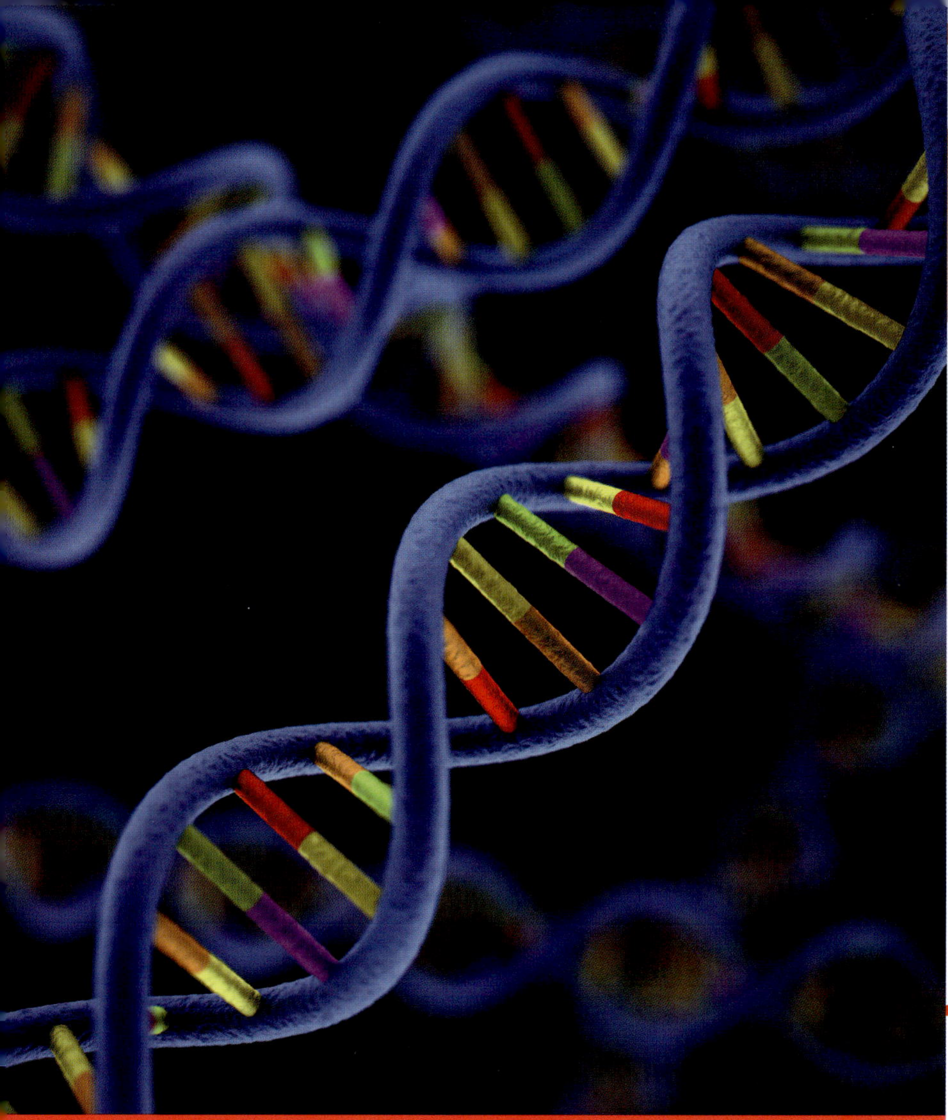

Scientists are confident about a genetic link with ADHD, though research about the exact nature of that connection is ongoing.

caused mostly by genetics, the actual genes, and the number of genes involved, are still unknown. In addition, the presumed environmental causes have not yet been proven. Assumptions are made about these causes based only on correlations. The evidence for these environmental factors has been inconsistent in some cases. Thus, scientists and public health officials will be working hard to collect more data on the condition's causes and risk factors. Future studies will explore the causes further and find new answers to today's questions about ADHD.

"Food additives include artificial colors, artificial sweeteners and preservatives. There's no solid evidence that food additives cause attention-deficit/hyperactivity disorder (ADHD)."[5]

—David C. Agerter, MD, family physician and ADHD expert

Chapter Three

Diagnosing ADHD

Diagnosing ADHD is not easy. There are no specific tests for it, and the condition has many symptoms. Some symptoms can also signal other conditions, including anxiety, depression, sleep disorders, or learning disabilities. One of these conditions may either explain the child's symptoms better or occur along with ADHD. Thus, a diagnosis requires a comprehensive evaluation that rules out other possible causes and determines whether other conditions are also present. Parents, teachers, and other caregivers may note symptoms or behaviors, but they should not attempt to diagnose the child. ADHD must be diagnosed by a trained health-care provider. This may be a psychologist, pediatrician, psychiatrist, clinical social worker, or nurse practitioner.

Psychologists are among the health-care providers that patients can speak to in order to get an ADHD diagnosis.

The Evaluation Process

The evaluation used to diagnose ADHD is lengthy and involves several parts. One of these is a thorough history of the child's behavior and symptoms, obtained from parents, teachers, and sometimes from the child. Clinicians often use checklists to rate ADHD symptoms and to rule out other conditions. These checklists, along with clinical interviews with the parents, child, and teachers, help the clinician determine whether the child's symptoms and associated problems warrant a diagnosis. The evaluation should include the child's ability to function in all settings, including home, school, and social settings, and his or her emotional functioning.

> "ADHD cannot yet be diagnosed in an individual child using brain imaging like MRI, PET or CT."[1]
>
> *—Leslie A. Hulvershorn, MD, child psychiatry researcher*

The evaluation process is similar in adults. The clinician gathers information from various family members and others who know the person well. He or she also uses checklists, behavior rating scales, a detailed history of the person's functioning in different settings, and an analysis of symptoms that

Many kids are diagnosed with ADHD while they are still in elementary school.

might suggest other conditions. In addition, the adult should have hearing and vision tests and possibly also a thyroid test to rule out other medical problems. Finally, the adult's childhood behavior and academic success should be considered. Since ADHD is largely genetic, the first symptoms appear in childhood, approximately before age 12.

Guidelines for ADHD Diagnosis

An ADHD diagnosis is based on guidelines given in the latest edition of the American Psychiatric Association's *Diagnostic and Statistical Manual of Mental Disorders* (*DSM-5*). These guidelines are used across the medical community to ensure that diagnoses are valid and consistent. To be diagnosed with ADHD, a person must show a consistent pattern of behavior over a period of at least six months. This behavior must interfere with the person's development or daily functioning.

There are many symptoms of ADHD, and they may vary among individuals. Three types of ADHD are recognized, depending on which symptoms are strongest. The first is a predominantly inattentive presentation, which describes people who have trouble paying attention, sticking to tasks, noticing details, or following instructions. The second is a predominantly hyperactive-impulsive presentation, which describes people who are fidgety, restless, or move excessively. They may have trouble controlling their actions, they may interrupt or grab things, and they may have more accidents and injuries than kids without ADHD. Finally, a combined presentation describes those who have symptoms of both of

The DSM-5

Mental health professionals use the *Diagnostic and Statistical Manual of Mental Disorders*, published by the American Psychiatric Association, to diagnose mental disorders, including ADHD. The *DSM*, first published in 1952, is now in its fifth revision (*DSM-5*), which was published in 2013. It is used in the United States to diagnose mental disorders and give treatment recommendations. It describes symptoms of each disorder and gives statistics on each, including the gender most affected, typical age of onset, common treatments, and effects of treatment. Mental health professionals also use the *DSM-5* to classify patients for billing purposes, and many insurance companies require a *DSM* diagnosis to approve payment.

the above. As children age, their symptoms and ADHD types can change.

Children age 16 and under must have at least six symptoms of ADHD for six months or more to be diagnosed. Adolescents age 17 and older and adults must have at least five symptoms for six months. The symptoms must be inappropriate for the person's developmental level, since some of them may be considered typical behavior for young children. For example, a child of ten might show impulsivity more characteristic of a child of six or seven. In addition to symptoms, other conditions must be met: several symptoms must have been present before age 12; several symptoms must be present

ADHD—Girls vs. Boys

Because ADHD presents differently based on gender, girls with ADHD may be overlooked. Boys are often impulsive, hyperactive, and physically aggressive. Girls more often have symptoms of inattention. Girls who do have hyperactive-impulsive symptoms may be seen as pushy, aggressive, or overemotional, or as talking too much. These behaviors in girls are more likely to be seen as a personality problem, whereas in boys, the same behavior might lead to a diagnosis of ADHD. Over time, failure to diagnose ADHD in girls may lead to academic and social problems, mental health issues, and lower self-esteem.

in two or more settings (home, school, work, or other); the symptoms must clearly interfere with the person's functioning in these settings; and the symptoms must not be explained by another cause, such as another mental condition.

From Child to Adult

Symptoms of ADHD appear in childhood, sometimes early childhood. But diagnosing ADHD is difficult both in children under four, who are changing rapidly, and in adolescent children. The type of ADHD may change as a child ages. In young children, symptoms of impulsivity and hyperactivity are most common. During the elementary school years, inattention symptoms may increase, causing a child to have difficulty in school. Adolescents may show fewer symptoms, but impulsiveness and inattention are often common, along with feelings of restlessness, relationship problems, and sometimes antisocial behaviors. The symptoms of inattention, impulsivity, and restlessness continue in adults.

> "Girls with ADHD tend to cluster in the inattentive subtype. Even those who exhibit more of the hyperactive-impulsive symptoms don't necessarily fit the so-called 'classic' profile of ADHD."[2]
>
> *—Dr. Patricia Quinn, director of the National Resource Center for Girls and Women with ADHD*

Some people are not diagnosed with ADHD until they are adults. Often this happens when their own child is diagnosed and the parent recognizes the same symptoms in himself or herself. However, to be diagnosed in adulthood, the person's symptoms must have first appeared in childhood. In addition to the typical ADHD symptoms, adults with ADHD may be chronically late or forgetful, be disorganized and have difficulty finishing tasks, suffer from anxiety and low self-esteem, and have problems at work. These symptoms may, in turn, lead to emotional, social, and work-related problems.

The challenges of ADHD can continue into high school, college, and a person's career.

Is ADHD Overdiagnosed?

Matthew Smith, PhD, a history professor at the University of Strathclyde in Glasgow, Scotland, argues that ADHD is being overdiagnosed around the world. The condition was first described in the United States in the late 1950s, and since the 1960s, it has been the most widely diagnosed US childhood disorder. Diagnosis of ADHD has also increased rapidly around the world. Its diagnosis is very often accompanied by the prescription of psychiatric drugs, which has been beneficial to the worldwide pharmaceutical industry. A Brazilian research group found that 5.29 percent of the world's children are affected by ADHD and that the condition was evenly distributed around the world.[3] When rates varied greatly among countries,

When Should Adults Be Tested for ADHD?

Sometimes people fail to realize they have ADHD until they become adults. Adults with certain life problems may suffer from ADHD and not realize it. If those problems are present, they may be warning signs, indicating that testing for ADHD may be helpful. They include frequently performing poorly at work, losing jobs, failing to perform to the best of their abilities, forgetting to pay bills on time, procrastinating on necessary chores, missing scheduled appointments, being easily upset, or feeling constantly stressed.

Gretchen LeFever Watson

In the 1990s, Gretchen LeFever Watson, a clinical psychologist in Virginia, studied 30,000 Virginia children. She found that rates of ADHD varied greatly by school districts and that some school districts were greatly overdiagnosing it. In some districts, 28 percent of boys were diagnosed with ADHD by fifth grade, and in others, the younger children at a given grade level were twenty times more likely to be prescribed drugs for treating ADHD than older children at that grade level.[4] The study earned LeFever Watson a research grant from the CDC. Then, she was anonymously accused of fraud and placed on leave. Although an investigation found her completely innocent of fraud, she said the accusation suppressed her large set of data, which she said would have contributed to the protection of children through better ADHD treatment and diagnosis.

they said, this was due to variations in study methods. Smith points out that the Brazilian study was funded in part by the pharmaceutical company Eli Lilly, which makes ADHD drugs. He thinks social, cultural, and political factors in other countries are important in explaining the variations in rates of ADHD.

A 2017 study, which analyzed the findings of more than a dozen other studies, outlined several reasons why ADHD may be overdiagnosed in the United States. First is the problem of diagnosis. The study explains that doctors sometimes rely on guesswork and stereotypes and that only about 25 percent of pediatricians actually base their diagnoses on the *DSM-5* criteria.[5] The criteria themselves may contribute to the problem, because they fail to provide a way to exclude other medical conditions that resemble ADHD. In addition, the study found that boys are routinely overdiagnosed, since doctors weighted behavioral problems too heavily in their diagnoses, as are younger children in each school class, who show these behaviors because they are less emotionally mature than their older counterparts.

A proper ADHD diagnosis is based on criteria outlined in the *DSM-5*. It is based on behavioral traits which are assumed to have biological bases, and, despite concerns of overdiagnosis and other problems, medical professionals are committed to helping children and adults with this condition. The diagnostic process is complex and not perfect, but it is improving.

Chapter Four

Who Gets ADHD?

It is difficult to get a handle on how common ADHD is, either in the United States or in the world. Percentages of people with ADHD vary by the organization providing the figures, for several reasons. First, researchers use different techniques to determine percentages, resulting in differing values that cannot be easily compared. For example, some doctors may confuse ADHD symptoms with symptoms of other conditions, leading to overdiagnosis. Others may fail to diagnose ADHD when it exists, leading to underdiagnosis. Second, ADHD diagnoses have increased over the years. Some say this means the condition is new, a result of various aspects of modern life. Others say it has always existed but that today's doctors are more aware of it and have better diagnostic tools and a better understanding of the condition.

Statistically, a significant percentage of kids in any given school are likely to have been diagnosed with ADHD.

ADHD through the Life Span

ADHD is often diagnosed in childhood, and children appear to be the age group most affected by it. According to the ADD Resource Center, symptoms of ADHD usually appear between the ages of three and six, and the average age of ADHD diagnosis is seven.[1] Based on a 2016 survey by the CDC, about 9.4 percent of US children, or 6.1 million kids, have been diagnosed with ADHD. A 2013 CDC

ADHD in teens may lead to disputes and arguments with family members.

study showed a steady increase in the percentage of children diagnosed between ages four and 17. This percentage rose from 7.8 percent in 2003 to 9.5 percent in 2007 and 11 percent in 2012.[2]

ADHD is considered a chronic health condition. According to the 2013 CDC study, the rate of diagnosis in boys was 15.1 percent, whereas the rate in girls was 6.7 percent.[3] However, this does not necessarily mean that more boys than girls have the condition. Because ADHD presents differently in girls than in boys, girls are often not diagnosed. By adulthood, the prevalence in males and females is approximately the same. ADHD often appears in combination with another behavioral, mental, or emotional disorder.

"Teen drivers diagnosed with ADHD are more likely to be in a traffic accident, be issued traffic and moving violations, and engage in risky driving behaviors."[5]

—ADHD editorial board, ADDitude Magazine

The CDC found in its 2016 study that of 6.1 million children ages two to 17 diagnosed with ADHD, 3.3 million were young people aged 12 to 17.[4] Teens with ADHD often have more family conflict, especially with their parents, than those

Additional Disorders in Kids with ADHD[6]

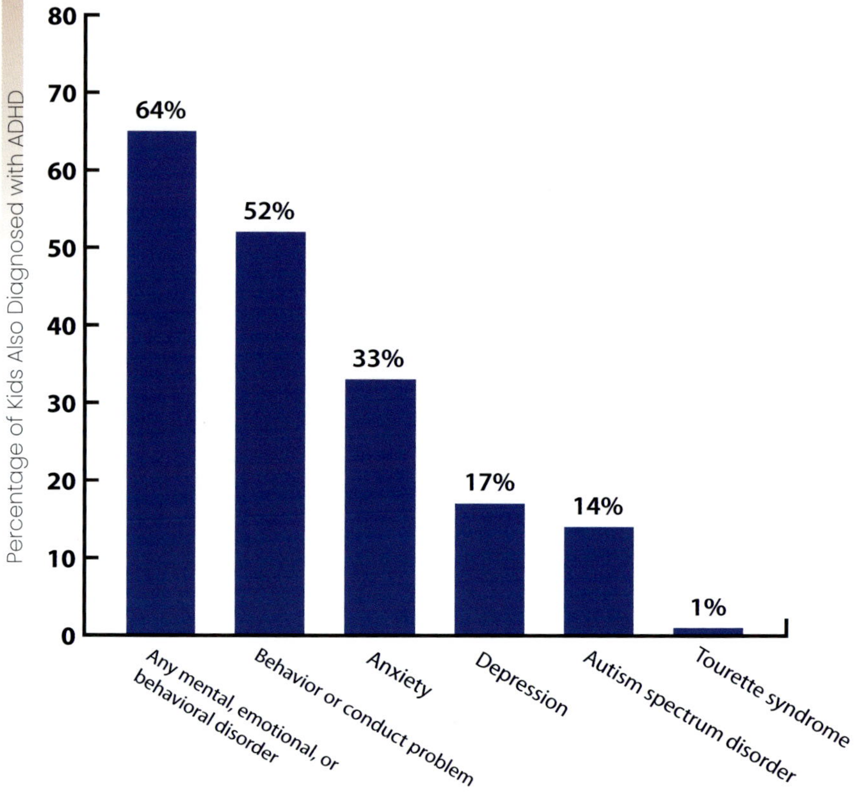

In 2016, more than 60 percent of children with ADHD also had another mental, emotional, or behavioral disorder. Slightly more than half had a disorder involving behavior or conduct, and about one-third suffered from anxiety.

without ADHD. In school, they have problems with attendance, grades, and homework, and they are more likely to fail courses and drop out. Teen drivers are also more at risk of accidents due to inattention and impulsivity.

Adults with ADHD are thought to make up approximately 2.5 percent of the world population; the value reported for the United States is 4.4 percent. However, the US value is thought to be low, as many adult ADHD cases may be unreported and untreated. Only 10.9 percent of adults diagnosed with the disorder are being treated. Scientists think adult ADHD may be underdiagnosed partly because the criteria were originally developed for children and partly because adults often have other psychiatric disorders that mask ADHD symptoms. Only about one-fourth of adults with the condition were diagnosed as children or teens. However, adult diagnoses of ADHD are growing four times faster than childhood diagnoses.[7]

ADHD Varies by Group

ADHD rates also vary among states and countries. Some US states—among them Alabama, Ohio, and Rhode Island—report more than 13 percent of children having ADHD. Others, such as California,

Studies have shown modest differences in ADHD diagnosis rates among kids of different races or ethnicities.

Colorado, and Nevada, report rates of 7 percent or less. Similar discrepancies occur in different countries. For example, Australia reports an ADHD rate of approximately 11 percent, while in the United Kingdom the reported rate is less than 3 percent.[8] These rates, however, may not reflect the actual rates of ADHD present. They may occur because of differing criteria for defining and diagnosing the disorder. They may also vary due to social and cultural factors, such as different definitions of "normal" behavior, access to quality mental health care, and the ability to pay for testing and treatment.

Two large surveys have been conducted that document, among other things, the rates of ADHD diagnosis by race or ethnicity. The National Health Interview Survey (NHIS), conducted between 2011 and 2013, found the following ADHD rates for children ages four to 17: 11.5 percent among non-Hispanic white kids, 8.9 percent among non-Hispanic Black kids, and 6.3 percent among Hispanic kids.[9] A more recent survey, the 2016 National Survey of Children's Health (NSCH), found the following rates for children ages two to 17: 8.4 percent among white kids, 10.7 percent among Black kids, 9.1 percent among non-Hispanic/Latino kids, 6.0 percent among Hispanic/Latino kids, and 6.6 percent among kids of other ethnicities.[10]

Economics appear to play a role in ADHD. Children whose families make less than twice the federal poverty level have an increased risk of suffering from the condition. Children whose households speak English are four times more likely to be diagnosed as those from non-English-speaking households. These statistics suggest that environmental factors may be very important in either developing or diagnosing ADHD, and perhaps both. But research into these factors has been limited, and the exact causes of these differences are not known.

ADHD and Public Health

The CDC sees ADHD as a serious public health issue. It is receiving new attention as the rates of ADHD diagnosis rise. In October 2019, the organization Children and Adults with Attention-Deficit/Hyperactivity Disorder (CHADD) hosted health-care professionals to discuss the issue. Among other things, they reported that ADHD individuals are more prone to medical conditions including accidental injury, cardiovascular disease, type 2 diabetes, and substance abuse. They are also at a higher risk for suicide. There is a significant reduction in life expectancy for people with ADHD—nine years lower on average for those diagnosed with ADHD as children, and 13 years lower on average if the disorder is still present at age 27.

Researchers have found that ADHD carries a high financial cost. According to a 2007 study, the average annual cost per person of having ADHD (the "cost of illness") was $14,576, and the total annual cost to people in the United States was approximately $42.5 billion.[11] This expense included diagnosis,

Famous People with ADHD

ADHD does not prevent people from having successful, fulfilling lives and careers. Many famous people report they have the disorder; they often say their success is helped by medication, family support, and structure in their lives. Sports stars with the disorder include Olympic gymnast Simone Biles, Olympic swimmer Michael Phelps, and NFL quarterback and analyst Terry Bradshaw. In the world of entertainment, singer Justin Timberlake, comedian Howie Mandel, rapper will.i.am, and Maroon 5 front man Adam Levine all report they have ADHD.

treatment plans, and medications. Related costs include education expenses, loss of income, and—in cases where the ADHD patient gets in trouble with the law—juvenile justice costs. In a 2012 study, researchers estimated an even higher total cost of ADHD to the nation, ranging from $143 billion to $266 billion.[12]

Some ADHD statistics may be depressing and even scary, but the news is not all bad. Though ADHD appears to be rising in the population, people with ADHD can not only learn to live with the condition but also learn to control it. They can go on to have highly successful, productive lives.

Chapter Five

The History of ADHD

While the disorder called ADHD has been recognized by that name for only a few decades, descriptions of ADHD-like behavior have been around for centuries. The earliest people to diagnose such a condition mentioned the patient's inability to focus, pay attention, or to stick to a task—still considered key symptoms of ADHD today. What has changed is the ability to describe the condition accurately, the understanding of its causes, and the methods of diagnosis and treatment. There has been an evolution in thinking about the condition as knowledge of medicine, the brain, and human behavior has advanced. As this understanding has become more refined, the condition has been

Sir Alexander Crichton, working in the late 1700s, was among the earliest physicians to publish descriptions of disorders related to inattention.

Earliest History of ADHD

Hippocrates, known as the father of modern medicine, lived in Greece from about 460 to 375 BCE. He described patients who were unable to focus on one thing for very long and who had very quick reactions to events—symptoms similar to those of ADHD. As treatment, he recommended drinking large amounts of water, doing physical exercise, and eating a bland diet high in fish. The next mention of an ADHD-like condition occurred in 1798 by Scottish physician Sir Alexander Crichton. He described people having "the disease of attention" as being mentally restless and having difficulty sticking to a single task. Around the same time, philosopher and physician John Locke described a group of students as unable to "keep their mind from straying."[1]

renamed over the years. The current name, ADHD, was accepted in 1987.

The Early Years

As he practiced medicine in several European cities, Scottish physician Sir Alexander Crichton became interested in mental illness, ultimately publishing three books detailing clinical cases. Book II, published in 1798, has a chapter called "On Attention and Its Diseases," which outlines a type of behavior that is consistent with inattention, one of the three primary symptoms defined as part of ADHD. He notes that the condition is often "born with a person," that it becomes evident very early in life, and that it "generally diminished with age."[2] He does not describe hyperactivity as part of the condition.

German physician Heinrich Hoffmann founded an advanced mental hospital in Frankfurt, Germany, and he was renowned for his efforts to improve treatment of psychiatric patients. But he may be best known for his children's stories, including "Zappelphilipp," or "Fidgety Phil," published in 1844. This story describes a small boy who is unable to sit still at the dinner table, eventually falling out of his chair and pulling the tablecloth and food off the table, an excellent description of hyperactivity. The boy also does not listen to his father, suggesting inattention, and the story implies that these are common occurrences, showing the persistence of symptoms over time. Finally, the story describes the parents' anger at Fidgety Phil, suggesting the family conflicts that often accompany the condition.

"Some . . . say that many famous people and historical figures could have had ADHD, such as Mozart, Leonardo da Vinci, or Ben Franklin."[3]

—Vincent Iannelli, MD, pediatrician

Previous Names for ADHD

Textbooks in the 1800s gave various names for the condition that today is called ADHD. These included nervous child, hypermetamorphosis, mental instability, unstable nervous system, and simple hyperexcitability. Later, terms such as minimal brain damage (or dysfunction or disorder), hyperactive child syndrome, or hyperkinesis were used. The second edition of the *DSM* (*DSM-II*), published in 1968, was the first to recognize ADHD, calling it hyperkinetic impulse disorder. The *DSM-III*, published in 1980, renamed it attention deficit disorder (ADD) and recognized two types: ADD with and without hyperactivity. Finally, a revised version of the *DSM-III*, published in 1987, changed the name to attention deficit hyperactivity disorder, which is still in use today.

Sir George Frederic Still, a British pediatrician, may be responsible for the scientific origin of the history of ADHD. Still gave a series of lectures in 1902 in which he described the condition now called ADHD as an "abnormal defect of moral control in children." He defined moral control as "the control of action in conformity with the idea of the good of all," and listed three factors on which it depends: "a cognitive relation to environment, moral consciousness, and volition."[4] Still said such lack of moral control was often seen in children with intellectual disabilities and in those with physical brain diseases, but he noted that other cases existed

In the early 1900s, Sir George Frederic Still helped lay the groundwork for the scientific study of what later became known as ADHD.

where the child did not suffer from such conditions. However, Still's concept does not specifically describe children with ADHD. Instead, it covers several categories of childhood behavior that include conduct disorder, oppositional defiant disorder, and learning disabilities. Probably only a few of the cases he described involved ADHD, and although he lists some signs of ADHD, those signs would not be sufficient to diagnose a child with the condition

PBD vs. ADHD

From 1917 to 1928, an epidemic of encephalitis lethargica affected 20 million people around the world.[5] This disease affects the brain, leaving the sufferer unable to speak or move. Many children survived the epidemic but then suffered from abnormal behavior. Their condition, named postencephalitic behavior disorder (PBD), caused a variety of symptoms, including emotional instability, cognitive and learning problems, tics, depression, and poor motor control. Children with PBD were often hyperactive, distractible, antisocial, and disruptive in school. Because many PBD symptoms are also found in children with ADHD, some doctors tried to correlate the two conditions. However, most of those affected by PBD would not have met the modern criteria for ADHD.

by today's standards. He pioneered the concept of childhood impulsivity that is distinguishable from both mental deficiency and physical disease.

Modern ADHD

In 1932, two German physicians, Franz Kramer and Hans Pollnow, described a childhood condition characterized by a marked restlessness. They called it "hyperkinetic disease." This condition is very similar to today's concept of ADHD. They described children as having an urgent motor activity, or inability to remain still, often running and climbing incessantly without a purpose or goal. The children could not complete tasks, answer questions, listen to instructions, or pay attention to details. These inabilities often led to disobedience and academic problems. Kramer and Pollnow's descriptions of hyperkinetic disease meet all three main symptoms of ADHD plus several additional criteria. It is the closest historical reference to the present-day concept of ADHD.

In 1937, Dr. Charles Bradley first used Benzedrine, a stimulant, to treat children with headaches, and he accidentally discovered its value for treating ADHD. But not until 1955 was there much interest in treating hyperactive disorders with drugs. At this time, several drugs became available for treating mental health issues, and research into the use of stimulants began. In 1957, three researchers—Maurice Laufer, Eric Denhoff, and Gerald Solomons—gave the name "hyperkinetic impulse disorder" to the condition now called ADHD. Laufer and Denhoff mentioned the stimulant Ritalin as a potential treatment for this disorder. The Food and Drug Administration (FDA) approved its use in children in 1961.

In the late 1960s and the 1970s, there was confusion and controversy over ADHD and its treatment. Due to widespread concern about drug abuse, Congress passed the Comprehensive Drug

Abuse Prevention and Control Act, which restricted the use of some drugs, including those used to treat ADHD. In 1975, Dr. Benjamin Feingold published a claim that ADHD is not a real diagnosis but rather a result of environmental factors such as diet. The media began to claim that stimulants such as Ritalin were dangerous and should not be used to treat children, causing a public outcry against using them. As research continued, evidence surfaced that these medicines weren't harmful. And, newer editions of the *DSM* gave more precise descriptions of ADHD. Both of these developments helped calm the controversy.

In the 1990s, clinical diagnoses of ADHD began to increase in the United States, and by 1991, prescriptions of Ritalin and amphetamines numbered in the millions. In 2000, the American Academy of Pediatrics (AAP) published guidelines for diagnosing childhood ADHD, and the next year it published treatment guidelines. It recommended behavior therapy combined with stimulant medication. In 2002, the first nonstimulant medication for ADHD, Strattera (atomoxetine) was approved by the FDA. There are now three FDA-approved nonstimulant medications for the disorder. The AAP updated both diagnosis and treatment guidelines in 2011.

Today, many people in the United States hold a purely biomedical view of ADHD. In other words, they consider it fully explainable by genetics and brain differences. Those in the United Kingdom point to "the interplay of multiple genetic and environmental factors."[6] These include not only exposure to lead and other toxins but psychosocial factors as well. Health historian Matthew Smith says such differences are typical when comparing US views of ADHD with those of other countries. Differences in cultural and political systems, he says, result in differences in how ADHD is perceived, diagnosed, and treated in various countries.

"Too often historical research on childhood disorders, such as ADHD, fails to keep the child central to the story. . . . Perhaps, instead of expecting all children, the world over, to conform to specific, *DSM*-determined criteria of behaviour, learning and development, we should do the opposite, and encourage creativity, courage and flexibility in our children, and in ourselves."[7]

—Matthew Smith, professor of health history, University of Strathclyde

Chapter *Six*

Dealing with ADHD at Home

It is often difficult for a child with ADHD to interact with parents and siblings. The family members are also affected. Family members often describe the experience as challenging and stressful. Unless the ADHD sufferer, parents, and siblings all learn techniques for managing this situation, it can result in conflicts, relationship problems, and generally less satisfaction with life. Fortunately, there are many behavioral strategies for children and adults that can help families remain happy and well-adjusted when a member is dealing with ADHD.

ADHD Challenges

Acting like typical children is difficult for those with ADHD, whatever their age. They may want to behave

ADHD can lead to clashes and disagreements within the family, but careful management of the disorder can help avoid some of these issues.

well and do what their parents ask, but often they just can't. They have too much energy and have difficulty controlling how they use that energy, sometimes resulting in disruptive or aggressive behavior. They are impulsive and overreact, responding to stressful situations with hair-trigger fight-or-flight behavior. They may argue or show anger and defiance. They have trouble with things such as keeping track of belongings and getting things done on time. Their approach to life is generally scattered, rather than organized. At the same time, their high spirits, passion, creativity, and boundless energy can make ADHD children exciting and fun to be around. But they must learn to manage ADHD behaviors so that ADHD traits can be expressed in a positive way.

> "Children with ADHD know what to do [but] they don't do what they know."[1]
>
> *—Lucy Jo Palladino, PhD, clinical psychologist*

Teens with ADHD likely recognize some of these characteristics. They know they are different, but they still want to be treated like everyone else, and as much as possible, be treated as adults. Among other things, this means taking responsibility for ADHD treatment, such as managing medication

How to Help Non-ADHD Siblings

Siblings of kids with ADHD often feel stressed and neglected because children with ADHD require so much time and effort from parents. Children with ADHD, in turn, may be so concerned with their own problems that they fail to realize how their behavior affects their siblings. Thus, parents must also make sure children without ADHD get the attention they need. They can schedule one-on-one time with these children, give them a safe place to express feelings, and let them know their feelings are understood. They can teach children without ADHD techniques for managing their feelings around the disorder, and they can be more understanding when siblings act out in response to the child with ADHD. Children with ADHD can also help by being aware of how their siblings are feeling and trying hard to follow rules and learn techniques to help control their ADHD.

and attending therapy sessions. But teens with ADHD may find that their parents and siblings have difficulty relating to them, and family life may become stressful. This is especially true if a family member, instead of accepting and respecting differences, sees them as bad or wrong. If this happens, someone with ADHD can feel inadequate and lacking in self-esteem.

Lack of communication and misunderstandings among family members can cause serious difficulties if not addressed. For example, a small study of siblings of kids with ADHD found that the majority of siblings felt their lives were seriously disrupted by the presence of the disorder. They said they never knew what to expect, and they described their lives as chaotic and exhausting. They felt that family life was focused on the child with ADHD, resented the time and attention lavished on that child, and also resented being asked to serve as caretakers for their siblings with ADHD. They craved a more typical family life, and they worried that the siblings' behavior would ruin or disrupt otherwise enjoyable events and activities.

Teens with ADHD may be able to address some of these potentially troublesome issues by communicating honestly with siblings. For example, teens might tell siblings how ADHD affects them and makes them feel. They might talk about working hard on learning techniques to control ADHD. One way to help family members understand how ADHD works and why people with ADHD act the way they do might be to share with them experiences of others who have the disorder, including people who are now famous and successful. Adam Levine, lead singer and songwriter for the band Maroon 5, was unable to complete tasks or sit still in class. He says he was diagnosed in his early teens and still has ADHD as an adult. His diagnosis, Levine says, came as a great

Openness and understanding between siblings can help stop conflicts before they happen.

relief because it gave him a better understanding of his difficulties. With supportive parents and a good treatment plan, he was able to begin controlling his symptoms. And now, in addition to a highly successful musical career, he has founded the "Own It" campaign, which helps children diagnosed with ADHD.

Managing the ADHD Family

Parents are often committed to helping kids with ADHD control their disorder. They will try to help kids learn to control inappropriate behaviors. They will try to make life easier for their kids, for themselves, and for the whole family. They may take parent training programs that teach strategies and behavior management techniques for dealing with a kid with ADHD. They may join a support group, such as a local group associated with CHADD, or seek advice from a medical professional. They may talk to siblings, babysitters, teachers, and other relatives to make sure everyone in the kid's life understands him or her, how to handle the differences in behavior, and what the rules and expectations are.

But caregivers are human; they make mistakes just as everyone does. Caregivers should never blame either themselves or their kids for having ADHD. The condition is primarily genetic. Its presence is no one's fault—it is a health condition, like asthma or diabetes, that must be managed. But a frustrated parent may seem to blame kids sometimes. Kids should understand this blame as frustration, and try not to take it personally—and of course, at all times, do their best to cooperate and work with their parents to control their ADHD. This will lead to a better outcome for the whole family.

It is important to maintain a positive attitude with regard to ADHD. This means teens should accept it

How Kids Can Help Manage Their ADHD Behavior

There are techniques ADHD kids can do as part of their daily routines to deal with ADHD characteristics such as hyperactivity, lack of focus, and impulsive behavior. Building exercise into the day's routine is a great help. This includes specific activities—such as running, swimming, and basketball—done every day at the same time. It also includes taking frequent breaks from homework or other quiet activities. Learning and regularly practicing relaxation and meditation techniques can help by calming a person with ADHD. Often, ADHD causes a person to be impulsive and blurt out things she or he didn't mean to say. Communication can help deal with this problem. Kids with ADHD can tell parents, siblings, and friends that they don't mean for this to happen. They can apologize if they say something hurtful, and they can work harder in the future to stop and think before acting or speaking.

as part of them and figure out the best way to manage it to make their lives, and their family members' lives, run smoothly. One way to do this is to concentrate on positive characteristics, such as high energy, creativity, or interpersonal skills. When people are aware that they are falling short in meeting parents' expectations—for example, they fail to clean their rooms or do their homework on time—they should not give up. They can ask their parents to help them try to find a solution to the situation. If both parents and kids are involved in developing solutions, the

"My child is destined for something wonderful, something that would be impossible for those calmer, regular-energy level children. I can think of several occupations where boundless energy would be an incredible asset."[3]

—Carol Barnier, parent of a child with ADHD

end results will be more satisfying. When parents give kids chances to take on more responsibility, the kids can do their best to live up to that faith. Usually, it is easiest to increase responsibility in small increments. This gives kids a chance to manage the tasks more easily and develop skills they can use throughout their lives. And as people solve problems and build skills, they will feel better about themselves.

Finally, if kids are taking medication, their parents should help ensure they take it regularly and responsibly. But the kids should not forget that they—not the medication—have ultimate control over their lives and behaviors. Sara Bykowski, mother of two ADHD sons, says, "I tell my kids that their medicine is like glasses. Glasses improve eyesight that the person already has. My kids know that their self-control, no matter how limited, is the main factor in their behavior management."[2]

ADHD and Nutrition

Poor diet and eating habits do not cause ADHD, and good diet does not control it—only medication and behavioral therapy or strategies do that. However, dietary changes can positively affect the lives of children with ADHD. This is because ADHD affects brain function, and good nutrition is necessary for good brain function. Proper nutrition improves

Parents and teens can work together to plan nutritious meals that are healthful for everyone in the family.

the functioning of three parts of the nervous system: brain cells, which process and transmit information electrically; the myelin sheath, which covers and insulates nerve cells and allows electrical impulses to travel quickly; and neurotransmitters, such as dopamine and serotonin, which transmit information chemically.

Brain function is enhanced by eating healthful, nutritious foods. Protein boosts alertness and decreases irritability. It provides the amino acids needed to make neurotransmitters. In general, carbohydrates decrease alertness and affect mood. Children with ADHD benefit from eating the right types of carbs—those with a low glycemic index (GI). The GI is a measure of the rate at which sugar from a food enters body cells. Foods with a high GI cause rapid production and release of insulin from the pancreas, which empties sugar quickly into the blood and then the cells. This makes blood sugar levels change rapidly, with corresponding ups and downs in behavior. Foods with a low GI even out insulin release and sugar uptake, which helps children with ADHD control their behavior. Finally, fats make up 60 percent of brain cells and nerves, but it is important to eat the right kinds of fats—particularly

What Should Children with ADHD Eat?

A good diet for those with ADHD includes proteins, fats, and the right kind of carbs. Protein is found in foods such as meat, eggs, cheese, beans, nuts, milk, and plain yogurt. Omega-6 and omega-3 fatty acids can be found in fish oil. Salmon and tuna are particularly rich in omega-3s. Other sources of omega-3s include wheat germ, walnuts, soybeans, eggs, and flaxseed and canola oils. Complex carbohydrates can be found in vegetables and some fruits, such as apples, cherries, grapes, oranges, and grapefruits. Whole fruits are better than juices; their fiber slows the uptake of sugars into the bloodstream. Citrus fruits should be avoided while on short-acting ADHD medications because their acids can interfere with absorption of the medication. Complex carbs also include high-fiber cereals, grains, and pastas.

two essential fatty acids found in fish oils, omega-3 and omega-6.[4]

Two studies from 2010 address the effects of diet on ADHD. One study concluded that organophosphate pesticides found on fruits and vegetables are linked to ADHD. The authors recommended eating organic foods, which are grown without such pesticides. The second study showed that a typical Western diet (one high in processed meats, fast foods, high-fat dairy products, and sugars) doubled the risk of an ADHD diagnosis. Although diet is neither a cause nor a cure for ADHD, good nutrition can make a difference.

Chapter *Seven*

ADHD at School and Work

Children, teens, and adults with ADHD face issues and challenges at home, school, and work. If they are fortunate enough to have family members and friends who are knowledgeable about ADHD and who help them learn to cope, they can have success in their daily lives. People with ADHD need support as they grow with the disorder, both in school and as they enter the workforce.

ADHD in the Classroom

There are many symptoms associated with ADHD, but those symptoms may indicate other disorders. Thus, teachers should observe a child carefully before recommending ADHD testing. Children with ADHD

Filled with potential distractions, the classroom can be a challenging environment for people with ADHD.

show inattention, impulsivity, and hyperactivity. But a child might be inattentive because she is anxious, is being bullied, or has dyslexia. Careful observation is essential. But when any of these symptoms are excessive for the child's age, and they cause ongoing problems, the teacher should alert parents. The parents can then get a thorough clinical evaluation by a psychologist to properly diagnose the child's behavior. Only then can the proper help be provided, giving the child a chance to escape the cycle of struggle and failure and start on the road to school success.

"Even as a kid, as early as 8, you know you can't do things that other people can do. And that takes a toll."[1]

—Dr. Patricia Quinn, director of the National Resource Center for Girls and Women with ADHD

Parent-teacher partnerships are essential for maximizing classroom success. Parents can participate by communicating regularly with the child's teacher. They can monitor the child to make sure he or she remembers homework assignments and completes them on time. They can ask the teacher for daily or weekly progress reports. Parents can be active advocates for their child with ADHD

IEPs and 504 Plans

Two laws relate to special services for kids with ADHD in school: the Individuals with Disabilities Education Act (IDEA) and Section 504 of the Rehabilitation Act of 1973. To receive help based on one of these plans, the child must meet the requirements for either an Individualized Education Program (IEP) or a 504 plan. An IEP provides individualized services to meet the child's unique needs. A 504 plan provides services and changes the learning environment to meet the child's needs. IEPs are for students who legally qualify for special education, while 504 plans are for those who don't qualify for special education but still have specific needs. Types of help offered by one or both of these plans might include extra time on tests, positive reinforcement, technology to help with tasks, help staying organized, or instruction tailored to the individual child.

by thoroughly understanding the child's ADHD and participating in the development of an IEP or 504 Plan, specialized plans that help educators tailor a child's education to her or his needs. They can keep careful records of their interactions with teachers and school administrators. Finally, they can ask questions and communicate concerns to remain fully informed about their child's school experience.

The teacher's role is difficult in part because each kid with ADHD is unique and strategies vary with each child. But some techniques are similar for all children. For example, all children with

Challenges for Girls with ADHD

Girls' ADHD symptoms are more subtle than boys', and they are more likely to be overlooked. Girls are less likely to be hyperactive and more likely to daydream. Girls with ADHD tend to turn their frustration inward and suffer more from depression, anxiety, or eating disorders. Because they are undiagnosed, they do not receive support and assistance from home or school. As teens they lack both social and academic skills, but they make strong efforts to fit in and succeed. They may appear successful on the outside, but this can come at great personal cost, including exhaustion and plummeting self-esteem. They are more likely to attempt suicide or self-harm. For researcher Rae Jacobson, who was undiagnosed until age 21, being diagnosed was a great relief: "It was something outside of myself, something I could understand, something I could plan for and manage."[2]

ADHD will likely benefit from a classroom with a predictable routine and short, simple rules. They will benefit from visual cues and reminders, such as video demonstrations of new skills and posted lists of important concepts. Other methods include encouraging active class participation and allowing for hands-on learning. Work should be at an appropriate level, and, if possible, ADHD students should be given choices for how to learn.

Teachers of those with ADHD must be patient, creative, and consistent. They must help students focus and learn to the best of their abilities.

Teachers can use a positive attitude to work to keep students with ADHD on track.

One especially important component of this is a positive attitude. The teacher can work with students to find ways to motivate them, figure out solutions to behavior problems, and provide praise for a job well done. Most successful programs for ADHD students involve three components: accommodations, instruction, and intervention. Accommodations involve setting up the classroom to make learning as easy as possible. Instruction involves using methods that kids with ADHD can master, and intervention means stopping disruptive behaviors before they distract other students or disrupt the classroom.

Two classroom management strategies have proven helpful for handling ADHD students. Behavioral classroom management concentrates on managing students' positive goal behaviors through a daily reward system. It is mostly used in elementary classrooms, but it can work at any age. In organizational skills interventions, students learn techniques such as time management, planning, and organization. Students use the skills in planning homework, organizing chores, and completing other real-life tasks to help positively reinforce the skills. These skills teach students to minimize distractions and improve learning. They are helpful at any age.

School Strategies

To deal with the unique needs of students with ADHD in the classroom, several techniques may help. Teachers can keep classroom rules and expectations clear, concise, and consistent. They can seat students who have ADHD away from sources of classroom distraction. They can also give immediate feedback on kids' behavior, whether good or bad, and make sure to reward good behavior. Teachers can give students with ADHD a chance to release energy, letting them move around, go get a drink, or do other things to curb restlessness.

One aspect that is often left out is the role of the kid with ADHD himself or herself. Much is said about the parent's and the teacher's role in the child's success. However, the child with ADHD must also be involved in determining strategies for success in school. The child with ADHD should continue to learn techniques for managing the condition. At the same time, she or he can become familiar with and apply basic strategies that aid success—for example, keeping rules written down and easily accessible, avoiding distractions by sitting at the front of the classroom, and asking for breaks when necessary. A student with ADHD can also benefit from tangible, practical tools. These include a school calendar, multiples of items the student often loses, highlighters for color-coding assignments by priority, and smartphone apps for tasks such as timing, scheduling, remembering due dates, setting priorities, and taking medication.

ADHD in the Workplace

After they leave school and enter the workforce, many adults with ADHD continue to struggle. If their ADHD symptoms are uncontrolled, they may have problems keeping a job. They may earn less than their peers because of their inability to concentrate, organize their work, or complete tasks on time. One study found that the difference among college graduates was an average of $4,300 per year.[3] Like their younger counterparts, they can overcome these problems if their ADHD is diagnosed, treated, and managed properly. It is also important to find the right kind of job. Some people find an active, on-the-go job is better suited to the ADHD mind than a quiet office job that involves sitting in a cubicle all day.

ADHD symptoms that prove challenging in the workplace, as in school, include distractibility, a short attention span, organization and memory problems, and restlessness. All of these can be managed using simple techniques. Distractions can be blocked out, for example, by finding a quiet workplace, closing the door, using headphones, and turning off email and text message alerts. It's possible to work with a short attention span by breaking large tasks into smaller segments, focusing for short but productive periods of time, and scheduling breaks. Time management skills are key. These include recording or taking notes in meetings, using a day planner to record deadlines, using visual timelines or checklists to keep track of deadlines and assignments, and setting phone alerts to help remember scheduled meetings or phone calls. Finally, people can channel their hyperactivity by scheduling frequent breaks, taking short walks

Channeling excess energy, such as by using a balance ball, is one way to manage the symptoms of ADHD at work.

around the office, visiting a coworker's desk rather than just emailing, or even keeping simple fitness equipment, such as a balance ball or hand weights, at their desks to burn excess energy. In short, it is possible to cope with ADHD both at school and at work, as long as the condition is well understood and a little advance planning is done. Many students and workers with ADHD are able to lead happy, productive, and fulfilling lives.

Working as a Teen with ADHD

ADHD teens can get practice in the workplace and learn to face the challenges of working with ADHD by working at summer jobs. It is always important for teens to look for jobs that suit them, and it is even more important if they have ADHD. Summer jobs help develop important life skills, including responsibility, communication, and social interaction. They help teens learn to follow directions and stay on task. Getting a job can be a job in itself. It is important for teens to look for jobs they will like and that will fit their skills. They should make sure to change their routines a week or two in advance, so they are prepared for the new hours required by the job. To succeed at work, people should dress appropriately,

> "The most important accommodation [for adult ADHD] isn't putting up a partition or getting the right lighting—it's finding the right job. . . . Think of your ideal career as the 'sweet spot' where three qualities intersect: what you love to do, what you're good at, and what you can get paid to do."[4]
>
> *—Edward Hallowell, MD, ADHD expert*

be punctual and polite, follow directions, and try to get along well with new coworkers.

According to Bob Seay of ADDitude, "The first rule of having a great job is to find something you would do for free and then figure out a way to get paid doing it."[5] If a person likes being at the pool, he could look for a job as a lifeguard or a swimming coach. If someone likes shopping, she could work in a retail store helping other people shop. If a teen likes animals, he could take care of other people's pets, or if he likes physical activity, he could work bagging groceries or making deliveries. Often, people with ADHD work best when working for themselves—for example, starting their own computer repair, lawn mowing, or home-cleaning businesses. In short, there is a world of jobs waiting for ADHD teens with drive, determination, and clear ideas of what they like to do.

Chapter Eight

Current Treatments for ADHD

There are two basic types of treatment for ADHD: behavioral therapy and medication. Often the two are used together. A precise treatment plan is usually developed for each individual. Treatment varies with age. For children under six, the AAP recommends that parents receive training in behavior management. As the child gets older, a combination of medication and therapy is recommended. For children up to age 12, therapy still includes training for parents. For adolescents, behavioral treatment often involves parents or other adults to help with reinforcing behavioral strategies or organizational skills. All behavioral treatments and medications must be used consistently, as long as the symptoms last. They are treatments, not cures.

Behavioral therapy is one proven, evidence-based treatment for ADHD.

Behavioral Treatment for ADHD

The goal of behavioral treatment for the ADHD individual is to help reduce disruptive behaviors and to learn and strengthen positive behaviors. It can help defuse tensions by helping the child with ADHD and his or her family overcome negative feelings and learn new skills and attitudes. This improves their ability to relate to one another.

"We don't have anything that keeps working after we stop doing it. . . . All treatments are what we call maintenance therapies, which means patients have to keep using them to keep getting the benefits."[1]

—Michael J. Kofler, PhD, director of the Children's Learning Clinic and an assistant professor at Florida State University

Among the types of behavioral therapy used in ADHD treatment are family therapy, training in parenting skills, and training in organization, planning, and time management skills. Family therapy can be used to help the child figure out how to minimize disruptive behaviors. Families and children learn to monitor and change their behaviors. They develop strategies and appropriate behaviors to use

Cognitive Behavioral Therapy

Cognitive behavioral therapy (CBT) is a type of therapy that covers topics such as mindfulness and acceptance, time management, problem-solving, and anger control. CBT is designed to help the ADHD individual respond with a more planned approach to thinking, behaving, and interacting socially. The individual should become more reflective, organized, and goal-oriented in carrying out everyday activities at home, at school, and in social situations. A controlled study measured the effect of CBT in a group of 119 adolescents with ADHD (ages 15 to 21) who combined CBT with medication.[2] Compared to control patients, those who received CBT showed significantly reduced ADHD symptoms and significantly reduced functional impairment. That is, they were able to function much more effectively after CBT. Several other studies have shown significant improvements in adults with ADHD receiving CBT treatments.

in specific situations. Behavioral treatment is often done with the child, a caregiver, and perhaps the child's teacher.

ADHD Medications

One of two classes of medications are usually prescribed for treatment of ADHD: stimulants and nonstimulants. Central nervous system (CNS) stimulants are the most often prescribed ADHD drugs. They increase the amounts of dopamine and norepinephrine produced by the brain. These neurotransmitters improve the patient's focus and concentration by helping the brain control its nerve impulses. There are many CNS stimulants that are best known by their brand names. All have similar chemicals as their active ingredients. Some of the more common stimulant types are amphetamine-based (including Adderall, Dexedrine, Dextrostat), dextromethamphetamine (including Desoxyn), dextromethylphenidate (including Focalin), and methylphenidate (including Concerta, Daytrana, Metadate, and Ritalin).

Certain types of nonstimulants have also been prescribed for ADHD treatment. Two of these, with the brand names Strattera and Pamelor, are thought to increase production of the neurotransmitter norepinephrine, thereby improving attention and memory. Two others, with the brand names Intuniv and Kapvay, are sometimes prescribed as well, although the exact way they work is not yet known. Experts believe they also affect the attention and memory centers of the brain.

Stimulants are prescribed most often, but some children do not tolerate them well, or they do not help with the child's ADHD symptoms. When these situations occur, the doctor may change the dosage, prescribe another stimulant, or switch to a nonstimulant. Stimulants and nonstimulants

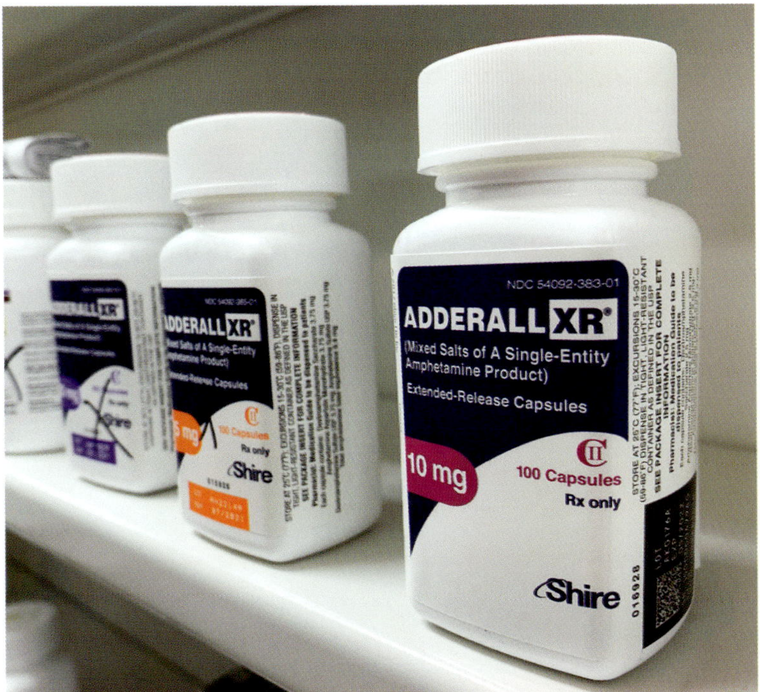

Adderall is among the stimulants used in treating ADHD.

have similar side effects, although stimulant side effects tend to be stronger. The most common include headaches, trouble sleeping, upset stomach, nervousness, decreased appetite, and dry mouth. In rare situations, stimulants may cause high blood pressure, hallucinations, allergic reactions, or even suicidal thoughts or actions. Nonstimulants can rarely cause seizures or suicidal thoughts or actions.

Antidepressants and ADHD

Antidepressant medications are sometimes prescribed for treatment of ADHD. They are sometimes prescribed along with stimulants, and they seem to help with all three aspects of ADHD—inattention, impulsivity, and hyperactivity. They work well for children who do not improve when using a stimulant alone, and they have also been effective for those who also suffer from depression or anxiety. Types of antidepressants used include tricyclics, such as Norpramin, Tofranil, Aventyl, and Pamelor, and selective serotonin reuptake inhibitors (SSRIs), such as Lexapro and Zoloft. Two other drugs sometimes used are bupropion (Wellbutrin) and venlafaxine (Effexor).

Non-Medication Treatments

Relaxation techniques, such as mindfulness meditation and yoga, can calm the mind. This increases attention and focus, and it decreases negative emotions such as impulsivity, depression, and anxiety. Mindfulness meditation relaxes a person and centers one's thoughts. It affects the brain's prefrontal cortex, which controls planning, attentiveness, and impulse control. It acts in ways that oppose ADHD's symptoms. Meditation can improve attention span and focus one's mind in order to limit distractions. It also improves emotional control.

Yoga, tai chi, and similar activities combine the psychological benefits of exercise and meditation.

Techniques involve deep breathing and attaining and holding physical positions for long time periods. These can help a person improve balance and stillness. These activities are not evidence-supported treatments for ADHD, but many people find the relaxation they provide to be valuable.

> "We haven't yet found the treatment that works for 100 percent of people. . . . Even well-established stimulant medications only help about 90 percent of people."[3]
>
> *—L. Eugene Arnold, MD, MEd, CHADD expert on ADHD*

Treating Adult ADHD

As with children, a combination of medication and behavioral therapy is a standard treatment for adults with ADHD. However, doctors caution that medication is not a cure-all. It does not work for everyone, and each person responds to it differently. Also, medication often has little effect on some of the important symptoms in adults with ADHD, such as disorganization, poor time management, procrastination, and forgetfulness. Various forms of therapy can be extremely helpful. Consulting a professional—a counselor, psychologist, or psychiatrist—can result in changing habits and

The eTNS System

In April 2019, the FDA approved the first medical device to treat ADHD. The device, called the eTNS, or external Trigeminal Nerve Stimulation System, can be used by ADHD patients ages seven to 12 who are not on medication. It is the size of a cell phone and connects through electrodes to a small patch attached to the patient's forehead. It is used at home during sleep, with a caregiver present. The eTNS generates a low electrical pulse that produces a tingling sensation. It sends nerve impulses to the trigeminal nerve, which connects to brain regions involved in regulating attention, emotion, and behavior. It may take up to four weeks to produce effects. Research on the real-world use of eTNS is ongoing, and the device is not yet widely available.

learning new skills that can transform the adult with ADHD. Cognitive behavioral therapy (CBT) can help the individual identify troublesome negative beliefs and behaviors and change these beliefs into positive, hopeful ones. It can also provide specific skills to help with disorganization, time management, and other current ADHD-related problems.

Simple techniques can have a profound effect on adults with ADHD. One important technique is regular exercise, which burns off excess energy, decreasing impulsivity. Exercise also boosts levels of the brain chemicals dopamine, norepinephrine, and serotonin, improving focus and attention. A second technique is getting plenty of sleep on a

Simple steps, such as good sleep habits, can help improve ADHD symptoms.

regular schedule. Adults with ADHD often have trouble sleeping. Keeping the room dark and quiet, with electronics turned off, for an hour or two before bedtime helps. Finally, a nutritious diet can improve ADHD symptoms. Meals and snacks should be regular, no more than three hours apart. The diet should contain healthful nutrients. Junk foods high in sugar and caffeine should be avoided.

Chapter
Nine

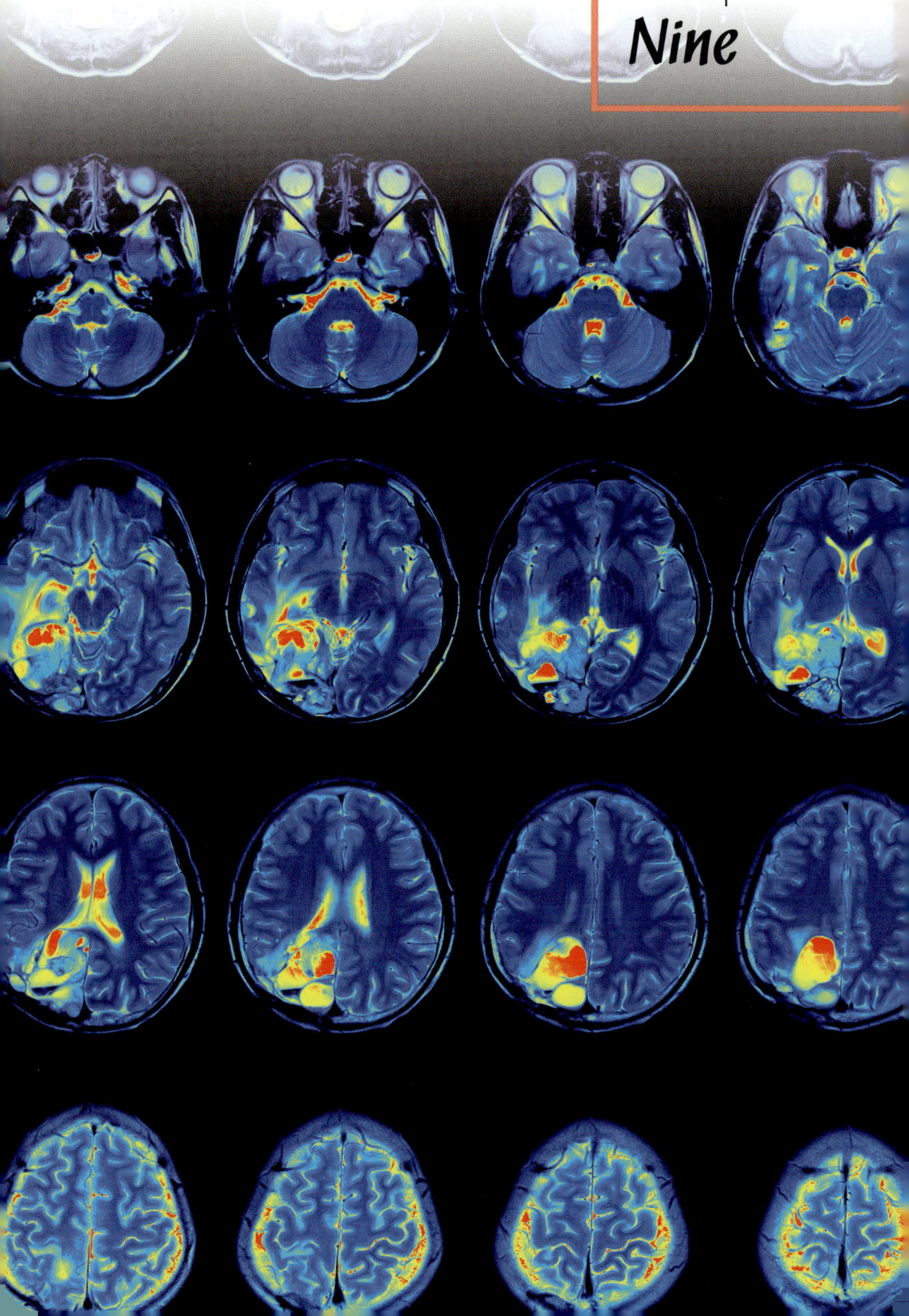

The Future of ADHD

ADHD has received relatively little study until the last few decades, and there is still much to learn about its causes, diagnosis, and potential treatments. Treatments, whether based on therapy or medication, have mostly been geared toward the management of ADHD symptoms and the associated problems those symptoms cause. But that is beginning to change, with some researchers now pursuing ideas that might lead to longer-term results.

Policy Research in ADHD

The CDC's Focus for the Future initiative provides families with tools and resources to provide the best care and support for kids with ADHD. The initiative also conducts research into national and community ADHD data on prevalence, treatments, and risk factors for ADHD. Additionally, it

Studying brain activity in people with ADHD may unlock more insight into how the disorder works and how best to treat it.

aims to raise parents' awareness of the newest information and resources available. The final aspect involves connecting families to the best available evidence-based treatment for ADHD.

There are still many questions about ADHD to be answered. People disagree about how many kids suffer from ADHD, what the characteristics and symptoms are, and what the likely future outcomes are. The CDC carries out several types of research to improve the understanding of ADHD in society. It does policy research to describe how various ADHD treatments are reimbursed by health plans such

The Future of Kids with ADHD

Chris A. Zeigler Dendy is a mental health professional who raised three kids with ADHD and now has five grandchildren with the condition. She has learned that kids with ADHD can be highly successful if their ADHD is properly treated. She has shared several key lessons. Dendy says that the best results come from early intervention. She notes that most teens face significant challenges but ultimately cope well. Dendy explains that a college degree is not essential to success, and she says most kids who have ADHD prefer hands-on careers with variety. Dendy also followed a group of 11 kids with ADHD through their late twenties. They are now succeeding in a variety of careers. The group includes a chef, a teacher, a minister, a bandleader, and an engineer who designs ejection seats for jets. Dendy says, "The final lesson my husband and I learned was to love our children unconditionally, just as they were."[1]

Web Tool for Doctors

Physicians are always looking for new tools to improve their ability to lessen the symptoms of kids with ADHD. One such tool is a web-based software program that pediatricians can use to see and evaluate reports from parents and teachers. Those who used the program saw larger drops in ADHD symptoms than those who did not use it. Parents, for example, said their children's symptoms were about 30 percent less severe when their pediatricians used the program.[2] The program helps doctors choose the most effective medications for kids who have ADHD. The program, called myADHDportal.com, was developed by Jeffrey Epstein, PhD, in 2016 at the Cincinnati Children's Hospital Medical Center.

as Medicaid. It analyzes health-care insurance claims data to understand how many people are seeking medication and psychological services. Some studies examine ADHD and co-occurring conditions, and others explore public health prevention and intervention strategies. Finally, the Project to Learn About ADHD in Youth (PLAY) study investigates the number of school-age children with ADHD, how the disorder develops over time, what other conditions and risks are involved, and what kinds of treatments are received. The PLAY study also looks at ADHD in diverse populations in an effort to learn what factors affect short- and long-term treatment outcomes.

All of these studies provide a basis for better understanding and future treatment of ADHD.

Cutting-Edge Research and Treatment

Research into the brains of those with ADHD is flourishing, and scientists are making advances. One line of research being carried out at the University of California, Los Angeles (UCLA) uses brain scans to test the effects of different medication regimens on children and teens ages seven to 14. The study has shown that a treatment in which two drugs—guanfacine and d-methylphenidate—are combined led to a greater improvement in attention than either drug alone. The brain scans showed evidence of effectiveness. The combined regimen appears safe, though it can have side effects, such as fainting. Doctors believe it has the potential for long-term benefits.

Scientists at the University of Mississippi Medical Center studied how hyperactivity in kids with ADHD affects their working memory. This aspect of memory involves the ability to process information and would be used when solving a math problem or answering a history question. In a study of 25 kids ages eight to 12, the scientists found that movement

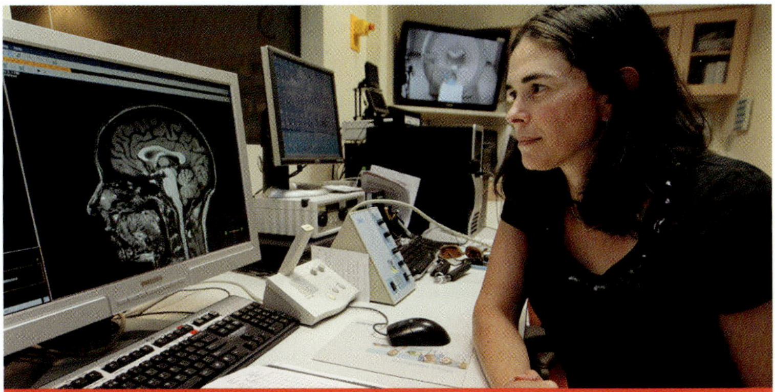

High-tech scans can help researchers better understand how to treat ADHD and other brain-based conditions.

improved their ability to remember and order small groups of random numbers and letters. Sometimes kids were told the number of items on a list; other times they weren't. They moved 25 percent more when they did not know the number, suggesting

Video Games as ADHD Treatment

A team headed by Dr. Michael J. Kofler is developing a video game to improve executive functions in kids with ADHD. These functions are centered in the brain's frontal and prefrontal areas. Kofler, his colleague Dr. Mark Rapport, clinical and cognitive psychologists, and games researchers are collaborating to develop the game. Early indications were that the video game works as well as or better than parent training. In future research, they will do 12-week trials, followed a few months later by tests to see how much of the gain in executive function is retained by the children. Researchers hope the video game will ultimately produce long-lasting benefits.

Pharmacogenomics

Pharmacogenomics is the study of how genes affect drug actions. This relatively new research field shows promise for developing new drugs to treat ADHD. By studying genomes, or individuals' complete genetic maps, scientists learn how different drugs influence patients and how to avoid adverse drug reactions. Such studies can also lead to personalized treatment regimens for different conditions. Scientists have identified nine genes associated with ADHD and related conditions involving the cardiovascular, immune, and nervous systems. Drugs currently being studied for use on these other conditions are potentially useful for ADHD treatment. For example, one drug currently used to treat symptoms of multiple sclerosis targets the same gene as one associated with ADHD, and it may eventually be used to improve cognitive skills in ADHD patients.

that hyperactive behavior may be purposeful—that is, it may help in the learning process.[3] Florida State University researchers led by Dr. Michael Kofler are investigating nondrug treatments to improve working memory in ADHD patients. Some of these treatments involve movement.

Other studies deal with ways to motivate ADHD individuals—both kids and adults—to carry out learning tasks. One study found that 20 minutes on an exercise bike made ADHD individuals more energetic and motivated to take a stressful memory test, even though it did not improve their performance. In a study of kids ages nine to 12, those with ADHD were more motivated than those without the disorder when they were given points for improvement. The rewards caused them to work harder and improve their performance on both memory and reaction-time tests. These results are based on early research, but they suggest that very simple techniques might be valuable in future treatment of ADHD.

Techniques such as brain scans, combined medication regimens, and nondrug treatments are opening up new avenues for the study of ADHD. As research progresses, the questions scientists ask are becoming more precise. For example, are different treatment regimens best for different groups of patients—for example, boys and girls? How do income, family stresses, environment, and other factors affect the outcomes of different treatment regimens? Are there unknown distinctions between different types of ADHD, and if so, do these different types respond to different treatments? Other important questions involve understanding the long-term outcomes of ADHD and analyzing ADHD in adults. Answers to questions like these could result in more targeted, precise, and individualized treatments for ADHD patients.

The Upside of ADHD

ADHD is a medical condition that must be managed throughout life. There is a tendency for people to consider it a negative part of their lives, something to be tolerated and dealt with but not appreciated. But many people are finding that ADHD can be very positive. People with ADHD, as well as ADHD experts, are learning to look for the upsides in having this condition, and there are many.

> "Our daughter's nicknames are Electric Sunshine and Fizzy Izzy. Her smile, her personality, her love of all people and animals always lights up a room. People are drawn to her positive attitude, continual stream of fun ideas, and fearlessness."[4]
>
> *—G. T. Thomas, parent of ADHD daughter*

People with ADHD may have trouble focusing and staying on task, but if they find a topic or activity that they love, they can become hyperfocused. They may channel all their energy in that direction and concentrate for many hours. This is what makes many scientists, writers, actors, musicians, and sports figures so successful—they practice constantly and they never quit. People with ADHD are often very versatile, and because they are impulsive, they react quickly. In an emergency, when quick action is required, a person with ADHD may be just who is needed.

> "Any of these deficits [of ADHD] can also be seen as strengths. . . . Consider how each can be used to your advantage."[5]
>
> *—Mayra Mendez, PhD, Providence Saint John's Child and Family Development Center*

People with ADHD are energetic, which is a tremendous asset if it can be focused on school, work, sports, or other important activities. ADHD individuals tend to be great problem solvers and to have great imagination and creativity—they often think outside the box. They notice fine details, including things other people miss. People with ADHD have numerous qualities that make them fun to be around and incredible assets in many situations. By seeking treatment to curb the downsides of the disorder and focusing on the potential upsides, people with ADHD are able to live happy, highly successful lives.

Essential Facts

Facts about ADHD

- ADHD is a brain-based medical condition that affects behavior by influencing how a person processes information.
- The three characteristic types of behaviors in ADHD are inattention, impulsivity, and hyperactivity.
- ADHD appears to be genetic in origin, but various environmental factors may cause or aggravate it, particularly exposure to toxins, alcohol, or drugs during pregnancy.
- About 9.4 percent of US children and 4.4 percent of adults have been diagnosed with ADHD. Diagnoses of adults have risen rapidly in recent years, possibly because of increased awareness of the disorder.

How ADHD Affects Daily Life

- People with ADHD often have difficulty navigating everyday life if the condition is not managed properly.
- Problems with inattention can cause trouble at school or work. People may have difficulty paying attention, noticing details, following instructions, and completing tasks.
- Those who are hyperactive cannot sit still, and they may tend to grab things or interrupt people. They are fidgety and restless, and they tend to have more accidents than people without ADHD.
- An inability to control impulses often leads to stress and confrontations with friends, family members, teachers, coworkers, and peers. This results in a chaotic living environment.

How ADHD Can Be Managed

- ADHD cannot be cured, but there are two general ways in which it is treated or managed: behavioral therapy and medication. The two are often used together.
- Therapy is designed to help the individual with ADHD reduce disruptive behaviors and enhance positive ones. Types of behavioral therapy include family therapy, skills interventions, and parenting skills training.
- The most common types of medications used to treat ADHD are stimulants, such as Ritalin, Benzedrine, and Adderall. A few nonstimulants have also been approved. The most commonly known are Strattera, Pamelor, Intuniv, and Kapvay.
- Relaxation techniques, such as mindfulness meditation and yoga, can sometimes be helpful in managing ADHD symptoms.

Quote

"The first step in helping a person with ADHD is understanding the origins of the condition. By understanding that these origins typically include genetic factors, people can become more objective about the condition and its effects, and blame doesn't have to be placed on parents or the person with ADHD."

—Kathleen Smith, PhD, licensed professional counselor

Glossary

causation
A situation in which one factor causes a change in another.

chronic
Continuing for a long time.

correlation
A close match between factors.

gene
A unit of hereditary information found in a chromosome.

hyperactivity
Excess activity.

impulsivity
Acting without thinking.

inattention
Difficulty paying attention.

neurotransmitter
A brain chemical that helps brain cells communicate with other brain cells.

pediatrician

A doctor who specializes in care for children.

pesticide

A substance or chemical used to destroy pests.

presentation

The way in which a disease or disorder makes itself visible in a person.

psychiatrist

A professional who specializes in diagnosing and treating mental health conditions.

psychologist

A person who specializes in the study of the mind.

psychosocial

Related to the interplay between society and an individual's thoughts and actions.

regimen

A routine or schedule.

toxin

A poison.

Additional Resources

Selected Bibliography

"Attention-Deficit/Hyperactivity Disorder." *Centers for Disease Control and Prevention*, 18 Apr. 2019, cdc.gov. Accessed 20 May 2020.

"Attention-Deficit/Hyperactivity Disorder." *National Institute of Mental Health*, Sept. 2019, nimh.nih.gov. Accessed 20 May 2020.

"What Is ADHD?" *American Psychiatric Association*, July 2017, psychiatry.org. Accessed 20 May 2020.

Further Readings

Mooney, Carla. *Academic Anxiety*. Abdo, 2022.

Mooney, Carla. *Teens and ADHD*. ReferencePoint, 2017.

Sanderson, Whitney. *Living with ADHD*. ReferencePoint, 2019.

Online Resources

Booklinks
NONFICTION NETWORK
FREE! ONLINE NONFICTION RESOURCES

To learn more about handling ADHD, please visit **abdobooklinks.com** or scan this QR code. These links are routinely monitored and updated to provide the most current information available.

More Information

For more information on this subject, contact or visit the following organizations:

Centers for Disease Control and Prevention (CDC)

US Department of Health & Human Services
1600 Clifton Rd.
Atlanta, GA 30329
900-232-4636
cdc.gov
The CDC is a major part of the US Department of Health & Human Services. It provides information and resources regarding a variety of conditions, including ADHD.

Children and Adults with Attention-Deficit/Hyperactivity Disorder (CHADD)

4221 Forbes Blvd., Ste. 270
Lanham, MD 20706
800-233-4050
chadd.org
The goal of CHADD is to improve the lives of children and adults with ADHD. It serves as a clearinghouse for information on ADHD, provides resources, and has local chapters that support individuals and families affected by ADHD.

Source Notes

CHAPTER 1. LIVING WITH ADHD

1. Blythe Grossberg, PsyD. "Inside Your Teen's ADHD Mind." *ADDitude*, 30 Oct. 2019, additudemag.com. Accessed 6 Aug. 2020.

2. "What Is ADHD?" *American Psychiatric Association*, July 2017, psychiatry.org. Accessed 6 Aug. 2020.

3. "ADHD Information for Teens." *CHADD*, 2020, chadd.org. Accessed 6 Aug. 2020.

4. "Data and Statistics about ADHD." *CDC*, 15 Oct. 2019, cdc.gov. Accessed 6 Aug. 2020.

5. "General Prevalence of ADHD." *CHADD*, 2020, chadd.org. Accessed 6 Aug. 2020.

CHAPTER 2. CAUSES OF ADHD

1. B. Franke et al. "The Genetics of Attention Deficit/Hyperactivity Disorder in Adults, a Review." *Nature: Molecular Psychiatry*, 22 Nov. 2011, nature.com. Accessed 6 Aug. 2020.

2. Kathleen Smith, PhD, LPC. "Causes of ADHD." *Psycom*, 12 Sept. 2019, psycom.net. Accessed 6 Aug. 2020.

3. "Causes of ADHD."

4. Kathleen Smith, PhD, LPC. "The Connection between ADHD and Bipolar Disorder." *Psycom*, 5 Oct. 2019, psycom.net. Accessed 6 Aug. 2020.

5. David C. Agerter. "ADHD Diet: Do Food Additives Cause Hyperactivity?" *Mayo Clinic*, 28 Sept. 2017, mayoclinic.org. Accessed 6 Aug. 2020.

CHAPTER 3. DIAGNOSING ADHD

1. Leslie A. Hulvershorn, MD, MSc. "How Is ADHD Diagnosed?" *Brain & Behavior Research Foundation*, 2020, bbrfoundation.org. Accessed 6 Aug. 2020.

2. Rae Jacobson. "How to Tell if Your Daughter Has ADHD." *Child Mind Institute*, 2020, childmind.org. Accessed 6 Aug. 2020.

3. Matthew Smith. "Hyperactive around the World? The History of ADHD in Global Perspective." *Social History of Medicine*, vol. 30, no. 4, 2017, pp. 767–787.

4. Pieter Cohen, MD, et al. "Is ADHD Overdiagnosed and Overtreated?" *Harvard Health Publishing*, 16 Mar. 2017, health.harvard.edu. Accessed 6 Aug. 2020.

5. Christopher Lane, PhD. "ADHD Is Now Widely Overdiagnosed and for Multiple Reasons." *Psychology Today*, 20 Oct. 2017, psychologytoday.com. Accessed 6 Aug. 2020.

CHAPTER 4. WHO GETS ADHD?

1. Kimberly Holland and Elsbeth Riley. "ADHD Numbers: Facts, Statistics, and You." *ADD Resource Center*, 11 Oct. 2017, addrc.org. Accessed 6 Aug. 2020.

2. "ADHD Statistics." *ADDitude*, 25 Feb. 2020, additudemag.com. Accessed 6 Aug. 2020.

3. "ADHD Statistics."

4. "ADHD Statistics."

5. "ADHD Statistics."

6. "Data and Statistics about ADHD." *CDC*, 15 Oct. 2019, cdc.gov. Accessed 6 Aug. 2020.

7. "ADHD Statistics."

8. Barbara Brody. "How Common Is ADHD?" *WebMD*, 12 Aug. 2015, webmd.com. Accessed 6 Aug. 2020.

9. "General Prevalence of ADHD." *CHADD*, 2020, chadd.org. Accessed 6 Aug. 2020.

10. "General Prevalence of ADHD."

11. Holland and Riley, "ADHD Numbers."

12. Jalpa A. Doshi, PhD, et al. "Economic Impact of Childhood and Adult Attention-Deficit/Hyperactivity Disorder in the United States." *Journal of the American Academy of Child & Adolescent Psychiatry.*, vol. 51, no. 10, 2012, pp. 990–1002.

CHAPTER 5. THE HISTORY OF ADHD

1. "More Fire than Water: A Short History of ADHD." *CHADD*, 4 Oct. 2018, chadd.org. Accessed 6 Aug. 2020.

2. Klaus W. Lange et al. "The History of Attention Deficit Hyperactivity Disorder." *Attention Deficit and Hyperactivity Disorders*, vol. 2, no. 4, pp. 241–255.

Source Notes *Continued*

3. Vincent Iannelli. "History and Medication Timeline of ADHD." *Verywell Mind*, 20 Feb. 2020, verywellmind.com. Accessed 6 Aug. 2020.

4. Lange et al., "History of Attention Deficit Hyperactivity Disorder."

5. Lange et al., "History of Attention Deficit Hyperactivity Disorder."

6. Matthew Smith. "Hyperactive around the World? The History of ADHD in Global Perspective." *Social History of Medicine*, vol. 30, no. 4, 2017, pp. 767–787.

7. Smith, "Hyperactive around the World?"

CHAPTER 6. DEALING WITH ADHD AT HOME

1. Margarita Tartakovsky. "Parenting Kids with ADHD: 16 Tips to Tackle Common Challenges." *Psych Central*, 8 Oct. 2018, psychcentral.com. Accessed 6 Aug. 2020.

2. Deborah Carpenter. "Never Punish a Child for Bad Behavior outside Their Control." *ADDitude*, 19 Sept. 2019, additudemag.com. Accessed 6 Aug. 2020.

3. Carpenter, "Bad Behavior outside Their Control."

4. "Change Your Diet, Find Your Focus." *ADDitude*, 30 Dec. 2019, additudemag.com. Accessed 6 Aug. 2020.

CHAPTER 7. ADHD AT SCHOOL AND WORK

1. Rae Jacobson. "How Girls with ADHD Are Different." *Child Mind Institute*, n.d., childmind.org. Accessed 6 Aug. 2020.

2. Jacobson, "How Girls with ADHD Are Different."

3. Royce Flippen. "ADHD at Work: Time Wasters and Productivity Killers." *ADDitude*, 21 Nov. 2019, additudemag.com. Accessed 6 Aug. 2020.

4. Peter Shankman and Edward Hallowell, MD. "9 to 5 with ADD: Practical Work Strategies for Clever ADHD Brains." *ADDitude*, 16 Oct. 2018, additudemag.com. Accessed 6 Aug. 2020.

5. Bob Seay. "Get a Head Start on Your Summer Job." *ADDitude*, 6 Oct. 2017, additudemag.com. Accessed 6 Aug. 2020.

CHAPTER 8. CURRENT TREATMENTS FOR ADHD

1. "Q&A: Video Game Holds Promise for Future of ADHD Treatment." *Healio*, 15 Feb. 2018, healio.com. Accessed 6 Aug. 2020.

2. "Cognitive Behavioral Therapy." *ADHD Institute*, n.d., adhd-institute.com. Accessed 6 Aug. 2020.

3. "New Device May Decrease Symptoms." *CHADD*, 2 May 2019, chadd.org. Accessed 6 Aug. 2020.

CHAPTER 9. THE FUTURE OF ADHD

1. Chris A. Zeigler Dendy, MS. "What Does the Future Hold for Our Children with ADHD?" *CHADD*, Aug. 2016, chadd.org. Accessed 6 Aug. 2020.

2. Sari Harrar. "ADHD Treatments: 5 Really Promising Research Updates." *Psycom*, 10 Jan. 2020, psycom.net. Accessed 6 Aug. 2020.

3. Harrar, "ADHD Treatments."

4. "What I Would Never Trade Away." *ADDitude*, n.d., additudemag.com. Accessed 6 Aug. 2020.

5. Stephanie Booth. "Reach Your Potential with Adult ADHD." *WebMD*, 8 Jan. 2018, webmd.com. Accessed 6 Aug. 2020.

Index

About the Author

Carol Hand

Carol Hand has a PhD in zoology. She has taught college biology, written biology assessments, written middle and high school science curricula, and authored more than 70 young adult science books, including several on health-related topics. Currently she works as a freelance science writer.

About the Consultant

Melissa R. Dvorsky, PhD

Melissa Dvorsky is a clinical psychologist at Children's National Hospital and assistant professor of psychiatry & behavioral health and pediatrics at George Washington University's School of Medicine and Health Sciences. Dr. Dvorsky's research studies the social, academic, and behavioral functioning of children, adolescents, and young adults with ADHD. Her work focuses on improving treatment for ADHD firstly by identifying and targeting risk and protective mechanisms and secondly by leveraging technology to personalize, disseminate, and sustain treatment. She is currently developing and piloting ATOM (Advanced Tools for Organization Management), a technology-enhanced behavioral intervention for adolescents with ADHD.